It's *You* I Like

A *Mister Rogers* Fill-In Book

You make each day a

special day when you

_____ .

You are happiest

when you're

_____ .

You were a great neighbor

when you

_____ .

I am proud of you

because you

_____ .

You made my heart sing

when you

_____ .

Having you in my life means

_____ .

You were as brave as

Lady Elaine when

_____ .

You help me feel at home

no matter where we are by

_____ .

Let's make the most

of a beautiful day by

_____ .

I love how curious you

are about

_____ .

The best idea you've

ever grown is

_____ .

You make everything in

life better by

_____ .

You taught me that

loving someone means

_____ .

You inspire me to be

myself when

_____ .

Even when we disagree, I know

I can always count on you to

_____ .

You've taught me the

importance of

_____ .

You face your fears when you

_____ .

You are your own person

because you

_____ .

I was glad you asked

for help when you

_____ .

You helped me find the

courage to grow by

_____ .

I know I can always

count on you to

_____ .

Something I learned about

you that surprised me was

_____ .

You helped me

understand that

_____ .

When I'm feeling down

you pick me up by

_____ .

Our friendship grew

stronger when

_____ .

I was so grateful to have

you by my side when

_____ .

I can always trust you to

_____.

The greatest gift you've

given me is

_____ .

The wisest thing you've

ever said to me was

_____ .

You see the best in the

world when you

_____ .

The best way you show

your love isn't through

words, it's through

_____ .

We've shared

_____,

_____

and

_____

together.

There's something so

unique about your

_____ .

In times of stress you

_____ .

You help me find

---

in even the smallest things.

You make music for others by

_____ .

You taught me that

neighbors are

_____ .

You show the strength of

King Friday XIII when you

_____ .

I hope you're proud of

yourself for all of the times you

_____ .

The most marvelous part

of life for you is

_____ .

You're my hero because

_____ .

The older I get, the more

I appreciate your

_____ .

You bring the good in life by

_____ .

You believe in

_____,

no matter what.

My wish for you is

_____ .

There's only one person

like you in the whole world,

_____ .

It's *you* I like.

RP Studio
Hachette Book Group
1290 Avenue of the Americas, New York, NY 10104
www.runningpress.com
@Running_Press

Printed in China

First Edition: October 2019

Published by RP Studio, an imprint of Perseus Books, LLC, a subsidiary of Hachette Book Group, Inc. The RP Studio name and logo is a trademark of the Hachette Book Group.

The publisher is not responsible for websites (or their content) that are not owned by the publisher.

Design by Rachel Peckman.

ISBN: 978-0-7624-9579-5

1010

10 9 8 7 6 5 4 3 2 1